Get Wise

The Environment
⊃ getting it right?

Sarah Medina

Heinemann
LIBRARY

www.heinemann.co.uk/library
Visit our website to find out more information about **Heinemann Library** books.

To order:
☎ Phone 44 (0) 1865 888066
📄 Send a fax to 44 (0) 1865 314091
💻 Visit the Heinemann Bookshop at www.heinemann.co.uk/library to browse our catalogue and order online.

First published in Great Britain by Heinemann Library, Halley Court, Jordan Hill, Oxford OX2 8EJ, part of Harcourt Education.

Heinemann is a registered trademark of Harcourt Education Ltd.

Editorial: Lucy Thunder and Helen Cannons
Design: David Poole and Kamae Design
Illustrations: Jeff Anderson
Picture Research: Rebecca Sodergren and Kay Altwegg
Production: Edward Moore

Originated by Repro Multi-Warna
Printed in China by WKT Company Limited

The paper used to print this book comes from sustainable resources.

ISBN 0 431 21002 0
08 07 06 05 04
10 9 8 7 6 5 4 3 2 1

British Library Cataloguing in Publication Data
Medina, Sarah
The environment – getting it right?. – (Get wise)
333.7
A full catalogue record for this book is available from the British Library.

Acknowledgements
The Publishers would like to thank the following for permission to reproduce photographs: Collection/Barry Payling p.**23**, /Paul Watts p.**18**; Corbis/Laura Dwight p.**8**, /Thom Lang p.**17**, /RF p.**12**; FLPA/Jurgen and Christine Johns p.**21**; Getty Images/Digital Vision p.**24**; Greenpeace p.**29**; NHPA/David Woodfall p.**25**; Panos Pictures/Neil Cooper p.**16**, /Jeremy Hartley p.**26**; Photofusion/Martin Bond pp.**13**, **27**, /Robert Brook pp.**6**, **10**, /Leslie Garland p.**11**, /Jo Lawbuary p.**22**, /Steve Morgan p.**19**, /John Tomkins p.**5**, /Bob Watkins p.**4**; RSPCA/Colin Seddon p.**20**; Zefa p.**15**.

Cover photograph of traffic scene, reproduced with permission of Powerstock.

Quotes and news items are taken from a variety of sources, including: BBC News, BBCi Newsround and the United Nations Pachamama website.

The Publishers would like to thank Glynnis Hendra, Advisory Teacher for PSHE and Citizenship, for her assistance in the preparation of this book.

Every effort has been made to contact copyright holders of any material reproduced in this book. Any omissions will be rectified in subsequent printings if notice is given to the Publishers.

Disclaimer

Contents

Words appearing in bold, **like this**, are explained in the Glossary.

Our home, the Earth

Do we look after the Earth as well as it looks after us?

The Earth is an amazing and beautiful place. It is full of variety – of plants and animals, mountains, rivers and oceans, which give us everything we need to live.

Great and small

Think about all the different places you have been to. Have you been to the seashore? To a river or lake? To a wood or forest? To your local park? All these places are different environments – with particular animals and plants that live there. Maybe you have seen crabs, fish or birds in some of the places you have visited – or oak trees, bluebells or dandelions? We talk about the environment on a larger scale, too, meaning the world around us – the world that gives us the air, water and food we need.

Fact Flash

So far, scientists have counted more than one million **species** of animals, but they think that there may be ten times this many. Who knows how many individual creatures this adds up to!

♦ When we think of the environment, we often think of the big picture – the whole world. We have local environments, too, such as this park in Greenwich in the middle of London. We have to look after these just as much.

↩ Have you ever been to the seaside? The sea is a very important environment – home to many thousands of different plants and animals.

All together now

All parts of the environment are linked to other parts in some way, in a delicate balance. Just think about a ladybird and its **food chain**. The rosebush needs air and water to grow. When it has grown, the greenfly eats its leaves – and along comes the ladybird and eats the greenfly. Like the rose bush, greenfly and the ladybird, we depend on the different parts of the environment for life.

Getting it right?

People have always taken the Earth for granted. For example, people cut down millions of trees, without stopping to think that many animals – and people – depend on trees to live. This lack of care means that water, land and air have all been damaged.

In recent years, however, people have woken up to the fact that we need to take care of our precious world – for ourselves and for the future. **Governments** and organizations have started to show people ways that they can help the environment. You can help, too! Even doing little things – such as using **recycled** paper – can make a big difference.

Top thoughts

'Young people are the driving force behind caring for the environment.'

David Bellamy, UK nature expert

What is the best way to take care of the Earth?

People use the Earth in different ways: for basic things, such as food, water and shelter; and for other activities, such as work and play. We either damage the world or protect it, depending on what we do each day.

Oil is used to produce many products, such as petrol and plastic. If we take too much oil from the Earth too quickly, there will not be enough left for people in the future. ◐

Talk time

How does what we do affect the world?

Tyrone: Well, my mum always tells me to switch off the lights when I leave a room. She says leaving them on wastes electricity.

Maribel: That's because we get a lot of electricity from burning coal, and coal might run out if we use it too quickly.

ali: Leaving the TV or CD player on standby wastes electricity, too.

Lauren: Water gets wasted, too – for example, if you leave the tap running while you clean your teeth. Or leave taps dripping...

Tyrone: Dropping litter is bad for the Earth. It looks ugly and it can even kill animals, if they try to eat it.

ali: Instead of throwing stuff away, we should **recycle** it. You can recycle loads of stuff – like paper, glass, aluminium and clothes.

For keeps?

Many people use the Earth without thinking about the future, in a way that is called 'unsustainable'. Unsustainable use of the Earth means that, although the Earth may provide what we need today, it will not be able to provide for people later on. Nowadays, many people are trying to use the Earth in a more **sustainable** way – that is, in a way that protects the Earth. They try not to waste anything, and they only use what they really need. They also try not to create **pollution**. By looking after the world this way, it will continue to look after us.

Newsflash

In a fantastic effort to care for the world, a youth group in Canada has developed an **organic** garden on an abandoned piece of land in the city of Vancouver. Their goal is to grow food in a sustainable way in a crowded city environment. The food they grow means they have to buy less. They also grow trees, flowers and herbs.

THINK IT THROUGH

Is the Earth our responsibility?

Yes. Humans affect the Earth more than any other thing. We should be careful how we use the Earth.

No. The Earth is here just to provide us with what we need. It doesn't need anything from us.

What do YOU think?

How well do you look after your local environment?

Think about where you live – your city, town or village. Your local environment is where you will find your home and school. What else is there? Perhaps there is a park or playground, fields, woodland or a river near by. We can get a lot of enjoyment from our local environment. By looking after it, we can make sure that others can enjoy it just as much, now and in the future.

TOP TIPS

Follow these top tips to help look after your local environment:

◎ Don't leave litter around – always put it in a bin.

◎ Instead of throwing away **organic matter**, like fruit and vegetable peelings, egg shells and teabags, make compost from them all.

♠ Organic matter, such as these peelings, can be made into compost in a compost bin. Compost is good for healthy soil – and healthy plants!

How Green Are You?

People who look after the environment are often called 'green'. Try this quiz to find out just how green you are!

On a piece of scrap paper, answer 'Always', 'Sometimes' or 'Never' to each of the following questions:

◎ Do you **recycle** paper, cans, clothes and glass?

◎ Do you re-use plastic bags when you go shopping?

◎ Do you switch the lights off when you leave a room?

◎ Do you turn off the TV or CD player when you are asleep or out?

◎ Do you have showers instead of baths, if you can?

◎ Do you leave the tap off whilst you clean your teeth?

◎ Do you walk or cycle to school?

◎ Do you build places for wild animals, such as birds, beetles and hedgehogs, to live in your garden or school field?

– Score 5 points for each time you answered 'Always'.
– Score 3 points for each time you answered 'Sometimes'.
– Score 0 points for each time you answered 'Never'.

Using your scrap paper, add up your total score – and see how green you are!

If you scored 36–40 points

Well done – you are very green indeed! You're really helping to look after the Earth. Keep up the good work!

If you scored 18–35 points

Pretty good – you are getting quite green! What you are doing is great, but you could try some of the other ideas here, too, to get even greener!

If you scored 0–17 points

Oh dear – you're not too green at all! There's lots more you can do to help look after the Earth. Don't worry – it isn't hard! Just have a go at the ideas mentioned in this book.

A load of rubbish?

What should we do with all the rubbish we produce?

Think about everything there is in your home and school – books, paper, TVs, computers, clothes, pens and pencils. At some stage, all these things become rubbish. **Recycling** and re-using them is much better than just throwing them away.

What a dump!

Billions of tonnes of rubbish are produced in the world every year. Most of it is dumped in landfill sites. These are large holes in the ground, which are covered over when they are full. Landfill sites are expensive and smelly – and they can spread disease. Rubbish is sometimes burned in special **incinerators**. The ashes that remain are then put into landfill sites. This takes up less room, but the smoke produced by burning the rubbish is not good for the environment, either.

Fact Flash

Every year, every family in the UK throws away six trees' worth of paper!

Cleaning up our act

Many countries now want to clean up their act when it comes to rubbish. In the UK, the **government** wants people to recycle 30 per cent of all their rubbish by 2010. We could do that today, just by recycling all our paper!

⬅ We are running out of space for landfill sites, like this one.

TOP TIPS

About 50 per cent of everything we use at home can be recycled. Most towns and villages have special recycling bins you can use. Try recycling these items:

◎ paper, card, newspapers and magazines
◎ glass bottles
◎ aluminium foil
◎ food and drink cans
◎ plastic bottles
◎ clothes.

🎧 Every tonne of recycled paper saves seventeen trees!

Talk time

How can we clean up our act?

Maribel: Well, we can stop buying things we don't really need.

Ali: And what we do need, we could make sure doesn't have loads of packaging.

Lauren: We could choose to buy recycled stuff, too.

Tyrone: Yeah, and take old shopping bags to put our shopping in.

Maribel: Or re-use stuff. Like, we could do swaps of old clothes and games.

Lauren: And music! Or we could take stuff we don't want to jumble sales or **charity** shops, so other people can use them.

THINK IT THROUGH

Is it good to 'shop until you drop'?

Yes. If I have the money to buy something, it's up to me.

No. We should only buy what we need. Every time someone makes something, it creates lots of rubbish – and we end up throwing things away, anyway.

What do YOU think?

The air we breathe

How can we keep our air fresh and clean?

Fact Flash

The oil we rely on, and which pollutes the air, is running out. There may only be enough oil left in the world to last another 50 years.

W e need clean air to lead healthy lives. Sadly, in many parts of the world, air **pollution** means that the air is far from clean.

Creature comforts

In countries such as the UK, the USA and Australia, most people are used to living comfortably. Heating keeps us warm and air-conditioning keeps us cool. We watch TV and listen to the radio. We travel in cars and aeroplanes. This modern way of living is only possible because of the vast amounts of energy we produce by burning fossil fuels – coal, oil and gas. However, there is a price to pay.

Paying the price

When we burn fossil fuels, poisonous gases are released into the **atmosphere**. Some of the gases fall back to the Earth in the form of **acid rain**, damaging trees and buildings, and killing wildlife. One gas, carbon dioxide, is causing **global warming**. The Earth's temperature is gradually increasing. Eventually, sea levels may rise, causing flooding in many parts of the world.

C Pollution from cars adds to the problem of global warming. Taking a bus is a much cleaner way of getting around.

A breath of fresh air

Many **governments** are trying to solve the problem of air pollution. In some cities, cars are banned when pollution levels are high. People are making machines that use less energy. Alternative, cleaner ways to produce electricity are being developed, including **solar power**, **wind power**, **wave power** and **hydro-electric power**.

There is lots you can do, too, to keep down air pollution. If you feel chilly, wear a jumper rather than turning the heating up. Always switch off lights when you don't need them. Never leave the tap running unnecessarily. And walk, or use buses or trains, instead of travelling in cars, which pollute the air really badly.

Newsflash

In 2003, London took a big step forward in keeping its air clean – by introducing a traffic congestion charge. On weekdays, people have to pay to drive in the city centre. It is hoped that the charge will reduce traffic by up to 15 per cent and cut traffic jams by up to 30 per cent. The money collected will go towards improving London's buses, trains and tubes.

Some people use solar power to heat and light up their homes. Solar panels take in the Sun's energy to make electricity.

THINK IT THROUGH

Is it worth paying more for cleaner ways to produce electricity?

Yes. We have to protect the Earth. We need cleaner electricity, even if it costs more.

No. People cannot afford to pay any more for their electricity.

What do YOU think?

The Earth is covered by a layer of special gas, called ozone, in the **atmosphere**. This 'ozone layer' has a very important job: it protects us from too many harmful rays from the Sun. This makes it possible for people, animals and plants to live safely.

Ozone hole

In 1984, scientists discovered a hole in the ozone layer over Antarctica. They realized that chemicals called **chlorofluorocarbons**, or CFCs, and **halons** were destroying the ozone layer – making it thinner and forming the hole. People were using these chemicals every day – in products such as air conditioners, fridges, aerosol sprays and fire extinguishers.

Damage to the ozone layer is not only bad for the environment – it is bad news for animals and people, too. If too many dangerous rays from the Sun reach the Earth, it can make it hard for people to fight off infections, such as colds and flu, and can cause eye problems and skin **cancer**. It can also make animals ill and die, too.

Hole no more!

In 1987, many countries signed an agreement called the Montreal Protocol. They agreed to reduce, and gradually ban, the use of CFCs and halons. This will allow the ozone layer to recover. Whilst a lot of progress has been made, there is more to be done before all countries stop using these dangerous chemicals completely.

We can all do our part, by making sure that the products we buy do not contain ozone-damaging chemicals. Any old products, such as fridges, should be thrown away properly, too. Your **local council** can help with this.

◖ Aerosol cans are used by millions of people everyday. In the UK, aerosols have not contained CFCs since 1989, so they are now safe for the environment.

THINK IT THROUGH

Is the ozone hole our fault?

Yes. It is because of our modern, comfortable lifestyles that the problem started. It's up to us now to look after the ozone layer.

No. We didn't mean to damage the ozone layer. Until recently, we didn't even know the damage that CFCs and halons could do.

What do YOU think?

How can we make sure that everyone has enough clean water?

Did you know that you could not live without water? It's true! You could survive for about 30 days without food – but you would die after just a few days without a drink.

No water, dirty water

In countries such as the UK, Australia and the USA, we may have plenty of clean, running water, but many people are not so fortunate. In some countries, especially in Africa, there is simply not enough fresh water to go round. As the world's **population** goes up, this problem will get worse.

◖ Some people, like these in Burkina Faso, Africa, have to walk for many miles every day to find water for drinking and washing.

Fact Flash

Having a bath uses 90 litres of water; taking a shower only uses 30 litres.

Talk time

What do we need water for?

 ali: For drinking, of course!

Tyrone: We use water for cooking, too.

 Maribel: We have showers and baths in water, and clean our teeth – and we flush the toilet with it!

Lauren: Our clothes get washed in water – and our dishes.

Water **pollution** is a problem in most countries. Water gets polluted because chemicals from **industry** and farming, or rubbish and **sewage**, are dumped in rivers. Every day, thousands of people in the world get ill – and 6000 children under the age of five die – because they have to drink dirty water.

Waste not, want not

Action is being taken by **governments** to improve the water problem. In many countries, there are laws against dumping chemicals in rivers, and industries have to use less water. **Charities**, such as WaterAid, help people in poor countries to build wells to find water.

You can make a difference, too. Try not to waste water. Never leave taps running when you clean your teeth, and always turn taps off tightly. Have showers instead of baths, if you can – or use less water in the bath. And collect rainwater in tubs to water plants in the garden or on the windowsill.

Newsflash

The **United Nations** (UN) has warned that the water problem could get worse unless urgent action is taken. The amount of clean water available for each person could fall by more than 30 per cent over the next 20 years, and 7 billion people could be without fresh water by 2050. The UN says that more must be done to cut pollution and waste.

🎧 A dripping tap wastes more water in one day than a person could drink in a week.

THINK IT THROUGH

Should people save water even when they have plenty?

Yes. Water is like everything else – it should be used in a **sustainable** way. People today need to make sure that people in the future will have enough.

No. Why save water if you're never going to run out?!

What do YOU think?

Sea world

What steps can we take to make sure that the sea stays clean?

Have you ever seen the sea? It seems to go on forever! In fact, three-quarters of the Earth is covered by the sea, and it is home to many thousands of varieties of animals and plants.

Fish farms

The sea holds a very important source of food: fish. Do you ever eat tuna sandwiches, smoked salmon, or cod and chips? These fish are caught in the sea. Fish is a very healthy food and, throughout the world, people eat more fish than they eat chicken, eggs, beef and lamb. Unfortunately, too much fishing (known as 'overfishing') has **endangered** many varieties of fish. The tuna, salmon, haddock and cod we love so much may soon run out – so we need to choose the fish we eat carefully!

Underwater rubbish

Think about the seaside towns you have visited. Millions of people visit the seaside every year – and more than half of the people in the world live near the sea. Sadly, where there are humans, there is rubbish. In one year, three times as much rubbish is dumped into the sea as the weight of the fish caught – causing serious damage to plant and animal life. It's not very nice to go to the seaside and swim in a sea full of rubbish, either!

Litter is ugly and dangerous to wildlife. Plastic bags can kill fish, which swallow them.

18

A fresh start

Countries around the world are starting to work together to look after the sea. Rules have been agreed about how many fish can be caught. This should mean that fish will recover from overfishing. There are also limits on how much rubbish can be dumped into the sea.

You can help to protect the sea, too. Remind your family and school not to buy fish that is endangered, such as cod and halibut. And remember to look after the seaside, for example, by keeping the beach free from litter.

Newsflash

In a major environmental disaster in 2002, the oil tanker *Prestige* split in two and sank in the sea near Spain, leaking 25,000 tonnes of oil into the water. Parts of the coasts of Spain, Portugal and France were **polluted** – damaging fish, shellfish and birds. Several European countries helped to clean up the oil from animals, plants and beaches.

In 1989, a big tanker ship called the *Exxon Valdez* spilled 35,000 tonnes of oil into the sea near Alaska. Some experts believe that the oil spill killed 250,000 birds, 2800 otters, 300 seals and 22 killer whales.

TOP TIPS

Follow the Coastal Code to protect rocky beaches, and the plants and animals that live there:

◎ Cause as little disturbance as possible. Always return rocks to the exact position and the same way up as you found them.

◎ Keep collections of live animals, such as shellfish, to a minimum.

Dying out

What can we do to save plants and animals from dying out?

Attract wildlife to your home or school! You only need a few flower pots to grow chrysanthemums – which butterflies love! And make little piles of wood to give hedgehogs and insects a perfect home. ◑

The world is full of plants and animals. Imagine sitting under a tree in the park on a hot summer's day – you would probably see buttercups and daisies on the grass, and birds and tiny insects all around you. Each type of plant or animal is called a **species** – and every single species has an important place in the world.

Going, going, gone...

Every day, between 30 and 70 species of plants and animals die out, or become **extinct**, because of things that people do. In the UK, even the hedgehog is in danger. Gardeners love hedgehogs, because they eat slugs and snails that damage plants. However, sometimes gardeners kill hedgehogs accidentally with lawnmowers or with poison that they use to kill slugs. More than anything, farmers have destroyed many of the places hedgehogs used to live, such as hedges.

Life savers

Governments and organizations across the world are now trying to save plants and animals from dying out. In the UK, the Wildlife and Countryside **Act** protects **endangered** animals from being killed, injured or disturbed. In Australia, the Environment Protection and Biodiversity Conservation Act protects animals and the places they live. There have been many successes. In 2002, a type of Australian stick insect thought to be extinct was found again.

Talk time

What can we do to help?

Lauren: We can support **charities** that protect animals, like the World Wide Fund for Nature.

Tyrone: Zoos help to protect endangered animals, too. You can 'adopt' an animal to help.

Maribel: We shouldn't buy stuff made with animal parts, like ornaments made from ivory from elephants.

ali: We can help to save trees, too – by **recycling** paper. That way, animals will still have somewhere to live.

Although otters had been dying out in ➡ some parts of the UK, they are now making a comeback. This is because people have been helping and protecting them.

THINK IT THROUGH

Do we need to protect species from extinction?

Yes. We depend on plants and animals for food and medicines.

No. There are millions of species, so it doesn't matter if a few die out.

What do YOU think?

Land for food

How should we look after the land we rely on?

Fact Flash

Half of the world's **population** live in towns and cities.

Where are you standing or sitting right now? In school? At home? In the library? Wherever you are, you are taking up a little bit of land. Land is very important – we build our homes, schools and shops on it. We need healthy land to grow the food we eat. Most plants and animals depend on healthy land, too.

Shrinking spaces

People are taking up more and more land. Today, there are six billion people in the world. By the time you are old, there may be nine billion! As towns and cities get bigger, we build more houses and roads – and there is less land for growing food. The land that is left has to work much harder.

People often use chemicals to make plants grow better – but this can **pollute** the soil, making the problem even worse. Land also needs to rest sometimes. In the UK, farmers often leave land to rest for a year at a time. In some countries, though, many people have to keep trying to grow their food on the same land, year after year. In the end, the land turns into desert – nothing can grow there any more. And so millions of people have to rely on other countries to send them food to eat.

⟲ One billion people in the world do not have enough food because their land has turned into desert.

Caring for land, caring for people

Many **governments**, and **charities** such as Oxfam, provide food for people who are hungry, and teach people to manage their land more carefully. Growing **organic** food protects land from pollution, because it does not use chemicals. Growing plants in a field for, say, one year and then letting the field rest for a year allows the soil to stay healthy. You can help care for land, too. You can even grow your own food! Potatoes, carrots and tomatoes can all be grown in containers. It's easy and fun – and it helps the environment!

🎧 When farmers look after their land carefully, healthy plants can grow for people and animals to eat.

Newsflash

In some countries, people cannot grow enough food. One UK family took part in a Red Cross project to see what it is like to eat only the amount of food given to starving people in Africa.

In a typical day, they ate some bread or a cinnamon bun for breakfast, bread with a bean paste for lunch, and pasta or vegetable soup for dinner – with just one portion of fruit and vegetables. Thirteen-year-old Mairead said 'It's easy for us to go back to the way we usually eat – but for some people in Africa, this is their only choice.'

THINK IT THROUGH

Should farmers use chemicals to help grow food?

Yes. Different chemicals protect plants from disease and from instects eating them – so farmers get better **crops**.

No. Chemicals can leak into the soil and polute it. They can also damage the environment.

What do YOU think?

Trees - the great providers

Why do we need trees – and how should we protect them?

We need trees! They provide food for people and animals, and shelter for many creatures. They store water and hold soil in place. And did you know that trees also help to make the oxygen that we need to breathe?

Chop, chop!

Thousands of years ago, 80 per cent of the UK was covered by forests. As the **population** grew, the trees were cut down – until only 4 per cent of the land was forest land. Cutting down large numbers of trees is called deforestation. People cut down trees to make room to grow food, to build roads and towns, and to sell wood.

Newsflash

Deforestation means that large areas of forests are disappearing quickly – and could be lost completely. Up to 40 per cent of the world's forests could disappear within 10–20 years. Forests in Russia and Indonesia are in particular danger. In Indonesia, deforestation causes serious problems for animals such as the orang-utan, which lives in the trees and is now at risk of becoming **extinct**.

Deforestation has serious effects. Many people depend on forests to survive, especially in countries with large forests, such as Brazil. Many animals need trees for food and shelter. When trees are cut down, the soil they grow in can get washed away by rain. Eventually, nothing can grow there.

The Amazon rainforest in South America will disappear in 100 years, if people keep cutting down the trees as they are today.

More trees, please

Many countries are protecting their forests by limiting how many trees can be cut down. They are also planting more trees, so that forest land can increase. In the UK, about 10 per cent of land is now covered by trees – much better than the 4 per cent there used to be. By **recycling** your old paper and buying recycled goods, you can help to save trees, too. You could also suggest planting a tree in your school or home, or join in with any tree-planting projects in your community.

Talk time

What are trees good for?

 Maribel: Trees give us healthy food – apples, plums, oranges...

 ali: And they provide wood for furniture.

Tyrone: Like chairs and beds...

Lauren: And things like pencils and paper, too.

 ali: Yeah, and they provide shelter for animals, such as birds and squirrels.

Maribel: And, on top of that, trees make the world more beautiful.

◖ Organizations such as the Tree Council in the UK plan tree-planting events, which everyone can take part in.

THINK IT THROUGH

Do we really need to save trees?

Yes. We need them for their food and wood, and for clean air.

No. We can get food from other places, and we can use other materials to make things.

What do YOU think?

How can people work together to help the environment?

We all know that we have to look after the Earth. We have taken it for granted for many years, and many people have finally realized the damage we have done – and are still doing. Countries across the world have agreed to work together to make things better. Lots has been done already – but there is still a great deal left to do.

Governments at the ➲ 2002 Earth Summit agreed to make fresh water available to all people. This new well is in Sierra Leone in Africa.

Newsflash

The UK government is thinking of protecting the environment by charging shoppers every time they use a new carrier bag. In the UK, people use 8 billion plastic bags every year – which is about 134 bags per person! They cause a lot of litter and pollution. The government wants people to **recycle** plastic bags. This is already happening in Ireland, where there was a 90 per cent drop in people using new carrier bags in just two months.

The big picture

Two 'Earth Summits', organized by the **United Nations**, brought people together to discuss the environment. In Brazil in 1992, 172 **governments** joined in – as well as 2400 other organizations. They agreed, for the first time, that we have a responsibility to live on the Earth in a **sustainable** way. Agreements were made to clean up the air, land and water. In South Africa in 2002, the second Earth Summit looked at what had been achieved so far – and came up with plans to do more.

Holding the key

Governments hold the key to improving the environment on a big scale. In the UK, the Department for Environment, Food and Rural Affairs (Defra) is responsible for protecting food, air, land, water, people, animals and plants. For example, Defra helps schools to teach children about the countryside and farming. Governments can also make **laws**, and can encourage **industry** to make products without causing **pollution**.

Many **charities** also work to protect the environment, including Friends of the Earth and Greenpeace. They put pressure on governments and industry to protect the Earth by making sure that they know what needs to be done. They also teach people about environmental issues.

◔ The UK government plans to use **wind power** as one of the main ways to produce the electricity we need to run our homes, schools and industry.

THINK IT THROUGH

Are the Earth Summits worth the time and money?

Yes. It is important for countries to meet to discuss problems and ideas. It might be slow, but at least there is some progress being made.

No. They're all talk. They don't make any real difference to the environment at all.

What do **YOU** think?

What can you do to look after the Earth?

You may think that environmental problems are far too big for you to solve. How can you sort out **global warming** and air **pollution**, just by yourself? How can you clean up all the rubbish that is dumped in the sea and on land? Or make sure that people look after animals land and trees properly? Of course, you can't do everything, alone. None of us can! But you can do little things that make a difference. And if we all do the little things, together, it will add up into something really huge!

Joining forces

All over the world, people are joining forces to help the environment. Some organizations have already been mentioned in this book. Their details are on page 31. Why don't you choose one you are interested in – and get in touch. There will be plenty you can do to help!

Top thoughts

'I am only one, but I am one. I cannot do everything, but still I can do something.'

Edward Everett Hale,
US writer
(1822–1909)

TOP TIPS

Here's a handy list of things you can do to help the environment at home, school and in the community. Go for it!

- Be interested! Learn as much as you can about the environment.

- **Recycle** books, papers, clothes, aluminium foil and cans, and glass bottles.

- Re-use whatever you can – swap clothes, books and CDs with friends, or take them to **charity** shops.

- Make **compost** from vegetable and fruit peelings, old teabags and egg shells, and garden rubbish.

- Don't buy products with too much packaging – it's a waste. And re-use old plastic bags when you go shopping.

- Don't waste water. Take showers instead of baths, don't leave taps running whilst you clean your teeth – and switch taps off properly. Get your family to only boil the amount of water that you really need, and only wash full loads of washing.

- Cut down on car journeys. Cycle or walk, or use public transport, such as buses.

- Never drop litter – and pick up and bin other people's litter when you can. You could even organize a 'Clean Up Litter Day' in your community.

- Save electricity! Don't leave lights, TVs or computers on when you are not using them. And get your family to wash clothes at a cooler temperature.

- Make a wildlife garden at home or school – and collect rainwater in pots to water it.

- Plant a tree – in your school, garden or community. And try growing your own vegetables, too.

- Always follow the Countryside Code when you are out and about – for example, by taking all your litter home with you.

Working with other people to help the environment is fun.

Glossary

acid rain rain or snow that contains damaging chemicals

act a kind of law

atmosphere layers of gases that surround and protect the Earth

cancer serious illness, which can kill people

charity organization that helps people in need and relies on money from the public

chlorofluorocarbons chemicals used in plastics, and to keep fridges, freezers and air conditioners cool

compost mixture of rotten organic matter, such as fruit and vegetable peelings, used to improve soil quality

crop grains, fruits and vegetables grown for food

endangered at risk of dying out (becoming extinct)

extinct when a plant or animal dies out completely. A species is said to be extinct if it has not been seen for 50 years.

food chain when plants or animals depend on other plants or animals for food, creating a chain – for example, foxes eat rabbits, which eat grass

global warming rise in the temperature of the Earth, which may cause sea levels to rise

government group of people who run a country

halons chemicals found in fire extinguishers

hydro-electric power use of water to produce electricity

incinerator special type of fire for burning rubbish

industry when products are made that people buy

law rule that a whole community or country has to follow

local council place where decisions are made and help is given for communities

organic grown without using damaging chemicals

organic matter substances that come from living things, such as fruit and vegetable peelings, other food leftovers (including egg shells and teabags) and garden rubbish

polluted/pollution when harmful substances, such as chemicals, damage air, land and water

population total number of people in a place or in the world

recycle re-use something, either by making something new from it, or by giving it away

sewage human waste that passes through toilets

solar power use of the Sun's rays to produce electricity

species type of plant or animal

sustainable way of living on the Earth that can last for a long time, because it limits what we take from the Earth to no more than we need

United Nations (also called the UN) an organization of 191 countries that works to make the world a safer and better place

wave power use of waves to produce electricity

wind power use of wind to produce electricity

Check it out

Check out these books and websites to find out more about the environment.

Books

Green Files: Future Power, Steve Parker (Heinemann, 2003)

Green Files: Waste and Recycling, Steve Parker (Heinemann, 2003)

Viewpoints: A Green World?, Nicola Baird (Franklin Watts, 2001)

What's At Issue? The Environment and You, (Alexander Gray, Heinemann, 2000)

Charities

Friends of the Earth (UK): www.foe.org.uk
   (Australia): www.foe.org.au
Greenpeace (UK): www.greenpeace.org.uk
   (Australia): www.greenpeace.org.au
Red Cross (UK): www.redcross.org.uk
   (Australia): www.redcross.org.au
Tree Council (UK): www.treecouncil.org.uk
WaterAid (UK): www.wateraid.org.uk
World Wide Fund for Nature (UK): www.wwf.org.uk
   (Australia): www.wwf.org.au
Young People's Trust for the Environment (UK):
   www.yptenc.org.uk

Other organizations

Countryside Code (UK):
   www.countryside.gov.uk/access/moreinfo_02.htm
United Nations Pachamama website:
   www.grida.no/geo2000/pacha/index.htm

Index

Titles in the *Get Wise* series:

Hardback   0 431 21003 9

Hardback   0 431 21004 7

Hardback   0 431 21002 0

Hardback   0 431 21000 4

Hardback   0 431 21001 2

Find out about other Heinemann library titles on our website www.heinemann.co.uk/library